LANDMARK TOP TENS

The World's Most Amazing
Pyramids

Ann Weil

Chicago, Illinois

www.heinemannraintree.com
Visit our website to find out
more information about
Heinemann-Raintree books.

To order:
☎ Phone 888-454-2279
💻 Visit www.heinemannraintree.com
    to browse our catalog and order online.

© 2012 Raintree
an imprint of Capstone Global Library, LLC
Chicago, Illinois

Customer Service: 888-454-2279
Visit our website at www.heinemannraintree.com

Edited by Megan Cotugno and Vaarunika Dharmapala
Designed by Victoria Allen
Picture research by Hannah Taylor and Ruth Blair
Illustrated by HL Studios and Oxford Designers
  and Illustrators
Original illustrations © Capstone Global Library Ltd (2011)
Production by Camilla Crask
Originated by Capstone Global Library Ltd
Printed in China by CTPS

15 14 13 12 11
10 9 8 7 6 5 4 3 2 1

Library of Congress Cataloging-in-Publication Data
Weil, Ann.
  The world's most amazing pyramids / Ann Weil.
    p. cm.—(Landmark top tens)
  Includes bibliographical references and index.
  ISBN 978-1-4109-4240-1 (hardcover)—ISBN 978-1-4109-
4251-7 (pbk.) 1. Pyramids—Egypt—Juvenile literature.
2. Pyramids—Central America—Juvenile literature. 3.
Pyramids—Juvenile literature. I. Title.
  DT63.W3 2012
  909—dc22   2010038403

Acknowledgments
The author and publishers are grateful to the following for
permission to reproduce copyright material: Alamy Images
pp. 7 (© Jim Henderson), 13 (© Robert Fried), 21 (© David
O. Bailey), 23 (© David Lyons), 24 (© F1online digitale
Bildagentur GmbH), 26 (© CuboImages srl), 19 (© Blaine
Harrington III); Corbis pp. 5 (Steven Vidler), 12 (Jean-Pierre
Lescourret), 22 (© John T. Young); Getty Images p. 27 (AFP/
ESSAM AL-SUDANI); istockphoto p. 4 (© Christopher
Russell); Photolibrary pp. 6 (Petr Svarc), 8 (JTB Photo), 18
(age fotostock/Maria Lourdes Alonso); Shutterstock pp. 9 (©
javarman), 10 (© Ian D Walker), 14 (© Dave Rock), 17 (© Gary
Yim), 20 (© tungtopgun), 25 (© Amra Pasic); The Art Archive
pp. 15, 16 (Museo Ciudad Mexico/Gianni Dagli Orti).

Cover photograph of Chichen Itza in Mexico reproduced with
permission of Shutterstock (© Drimi).

We would like to thank Daniel Block for his invaluable help in
the preparation of this book.

Every effort has been made to contact copyright holders of
material reproduced in this book. Any omissions will be
rectified in subsequent printings if notice is given to the
publisher.

Disclaimer
All the internet addresses (URLs) given in this book were valid
at the time of going to press. However, due to the dynamic
nature of the internet, some addresses may have changed, or
sites may have changed or ceased to exist since publication.
While the author and publisher regret any inconvenience this
may cause readers, no responsibility for any such changes can
be accepted by either the author or the publisher.

Contents

Some words are printed in bold, **like this**. You can find out
what they mean in the glossary.

Pyramids

Pyramids are some of the first large structures made by humans. Ancient cultures in different parts of the world built pyramids. In Egypt, pyramids were **tombs** for kings called **pharaohs**. Long ago people in Central America built pyramids with temples on top and used them for religious **rituals**.

Incredible Power

Imagine trying to build huge structures such as these without cranes or other modern building machinery. The Egyptians and Mayans did it all with human power!

This temple is the highest building at Tikal in Guatemala, and probably the tallest structure ever built by the ancient Mayan people. It stands about 213 feet (65 meters) high.

Cats were considered **sacred** animals in ancient Egypt. Killing a cat was punishable by death. Some cats were mummified after they died.

The afterlife

The ancient Egyptians believed that the afterlife was similar to everyday life. When a pharaoh died, his body was preserved by **mummification** so that his spirit would still have a home. Pyramids were grand houses for dead kings. Food, furniture, treasures, and even pets were buried with the dead so that they would be more comfortable in the afterlife.

Khufu's Pyramid

Ancient Egyptian kings called **pharaohs** designed and built pyramids, which would eventually become their own **tombs**. A pharaoh called Khufu ruled Egypt around 2500 BCE. Khufu's Pyramid is the largest ever built in Egypt.

Pyramids are triangle-shaped. King Khufu's pyramid was originally covered with smooth white stone. Over the years the outer layer of stones has been stolen.

**Khufu's Pyramid
(The Great Pyramid of Giza)**
Location: Giza, Egypt
Height: 481 feet (147 meters)
That's Amazing!
The Great Pyramid of Giza is the only one of the **Seven Wonders of the Ancient World** still standing today.

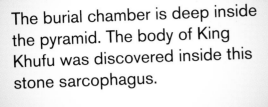

The burial chamber is deep inside the pyramid. The body of King Khufu was discovered inside this stone sarcophagus.

Amazing Facts

Number of stone blocks: Around 2.3 million

Original Height: 481 feet (147 meters)

Number of years to build: Around 23

Inside the pyramid

Egyptian pyramids have underground chambers. Khufu's Pyramid has a huge stone **sarcophagus** inside it.

Tunnels from some of the pyramid's chambers allow views of important stars. Experts think the tunnels were meant to help the spirit of the dead king find his way by the stars.

Djoser's (Zoser's) Pyramid

Khufu's **tomb** may be the biggest Egyptian pyramid, but it was not the first. King Djoser (or "Zoser") built a great pyramid 70 years earlier. Experts believe this was the first pyramid. Before Djoser's Pyramid, Egyptian tombs were mounds of mud bricks and sand. But these tombs did not last long. Wind and weather wore them down. King Djoser wanted his tomb to last, so he used stone blocks to create an enormous step pyramid.

Djoser's (Zoser's) Pyramid
Location: Saqqara, Egypt
Size: Originally 203 feet (62 meters) tall
That's Amazing!
This pyramid is the oldest stone building in Egypt.

Djoser's Pyramid has been listed as a **World Heritage Site**.

Sneferu's Pyramid Mistakes

Pharaoh Huni built a step pyramid in Meidun, Egypt. His son, Sneferu, added stones to make the sides smooth. But the new layer came crashing down, taking a lot of the original steps with it. Sneferu tried again. This time he began a straight-sided pyramid at Dahshur (above). The sides of this pyramid were very steep. Halfway up, he changed his mind about the slope. It is now known as the Bent Pyramid.

Pyramid of the Sun

The Pyramid of the Sun, near Mexico City, was built as a great temple. Human skeletons were found in each corner when the site was **excavated**. They were probably the victims of human **sacrifice**. Some ancient Mexican cultures believed that blood sacrifices maintained the balance of nature. But experts are not absolutely sure which ancient civilization created this amazing pyramid, so the original builders remain unknown.

The Pyramid of the Sun is the second largest pyramid in Central America.

Teotihuacán

The Pyramid of the Sun is the largest of three great pyramids in a huge, ancient city known as Teotihuacán. Around 500 CE as many as 200,000 people lived there. It was one of the largest cities in the world at that time.

Pyramid of the Sun

Location: Near Mexico City, Mexico

Height: 216 feet (66 meters)

That's Amazing!

It's the third-largest in the world, and the largest pyramid to be restored in the **Western Hemisphere.**

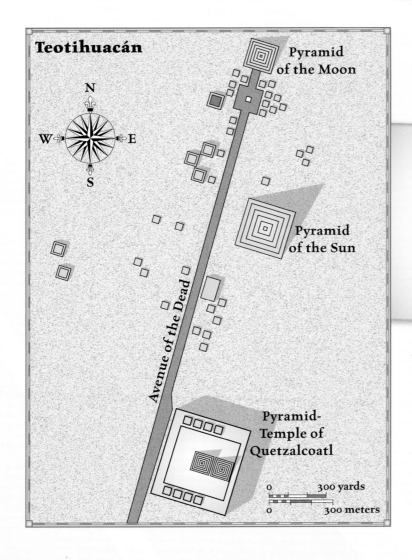

The city of Teotihuacán was abandoned in around 700 CE. Experts are still trying to figure out why the people left.

Pyramid of Kukulcán

Between the 11th and 13th centuries, the Mayans built this pyramid in honor of Kukulkán, one of the three gods they believed created the Earth. Kukulkán's natural form was a snake with wings. The god's human form was a tall, white-skinned man, with light hair and blue eyes. This image has puzzled experts because it looks like a European man. Mayan people were shorter with dark hair and eyes.

Pyramid of Kukulcán

Location: Chitchen Itza, Mexico

Height: Approximately 79 feet (24 meters)

That's Amazing!

This pyramid is also a huge stone calendar!

The Pyramid of Kukulcán is also called *El Castillo*, which means "the castle" in Spanish.

The Pyramid of Kukulcán is the largest pyramid in the ancient city of Chitchen Itza.

Ancient calendars

This pyramid's design reflects the Mayan calendar, which was similar to the one we use today. It was built with exactly 365 steps, the number of days in a year. Each of our seasons begins on a **solstice** or **equinox**. These days were special for the Mayans, too. On the day of the equinox the Sun creates the shadow of a snake on the side of this amazing pyramid!

Pyramid of Inscriptions

The Pyramid of **Inscriptions** in Mexico gets its name from the three stone tablets in the main chamber. These tablets are the longest Mayan inscriptions ever found. Mayan symbols are carved into the stone. They tell the history of the rulers of this city, up to Lord Pacal, who built this step pyramid for his own **tomb**.

Pyramid of Inscriptions
Location: Palenque, Chiapas, Mexico
Size: 197 feet (60 meters) wide and 89 feet (27 meters) tall

That's Amazing!
Experts studied this pyramid for 200 years before discovering the hidden tomb of a Mayan king.

This pyramid was an important building in the ancient Mayan city now known as Palenque.

Some experts think the carvings show Lord Pacal falling into the underworld. Others think it shows him emerging as a god.

Palenque

In 1949 workers at Palenque found a trap door in the floor of the pyramid's main chamber. Inside a hidden chamber was a gigantic carved stone coffin. They had discovered Lord Pacal's tomb! The remains of six human **sacrifices** lay near the coffin.

El Templo Mayor

The Aztec people dedicated El Templo Mayor ("the main temple"), a temple-pyramid, to their gods of war and water. The temple was built, destroyed, and rebuilt seven times over 200 years. When the sixth temple was completed, the Aztec ruler ordered a huge number of human **sacrifices**. About 2,000 prisoners of war were killed over a period of 20 days! The Aztecs believed that blood from human sacrifices kept their world alive and strong.

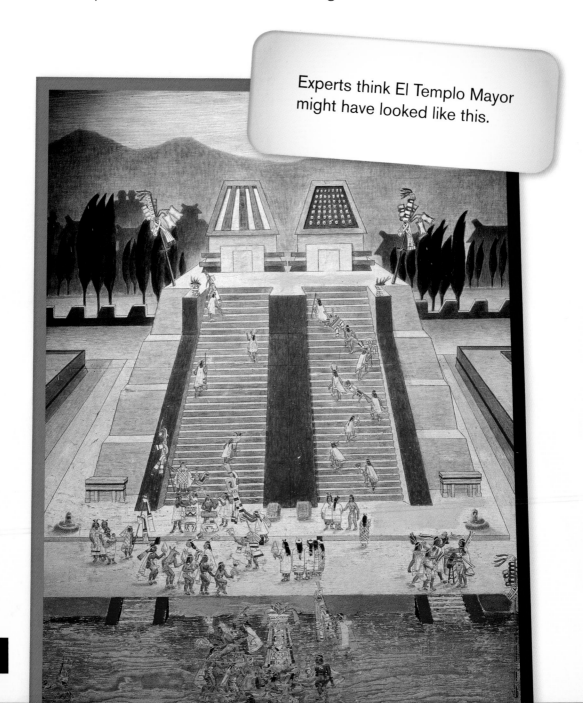

Experts think El Templo Mayor might have looked like this.

The Aztecs built this "Wall of Skulls" using real human heads covered with a kind of plaster called stucco.

El Templo Mayor

Location: Mexico City, Mexico

Size: Approximately 330 x 260 feet (100 x 80 meters) at its base

That's Amazing!

The Spanish destroyed this pyramid in 1521 and built a new city on top of the site.

Tenochtitlán

The Aztec people were the last great native civilization in Central America, and the last to build big pyramids. Tenochtitlán was their capital city. It was built on an island in Lake Texcoco. Modern-day Mexico City is built over this ancient city.

Los Guachimontones

In 1970 a Mexican husband-and-wife team found some of the most amazing pyramids in North America. Three circular pyramids were buried underneath hills where farmers had been growing crops for generations. Experts think the pyramids at Los Guachimontones were used for **rituals**, not as **tombs**. Based on what they found at the site, they believe that a very important priest tied himself to a pole using a long rope, and swung around like a tetherball!

Los Guachimontones
Location: Jalisco, Mexico
Height: 60 feet (18 meters)
That's Amazing!
This is the largest round pyramid in Mexico.

The pyramids at Los Guachimontones were hidden underground until recently.

The site of the Los Guachimontones pyramids is now carefully taken care of by the local people.

Ball games!

The pyramids at Los Guachimontones were part of a city that included ball courts. The ancient ball game was like soccer. The ball was probably a stone covered with rubber. Many male skeletons found near the site showed evidence of broken bones near their hips.

Louvre Pyramid

Most pyramids were built in ancient times, but the Louvre Pyramid in Paris was built in the 1980s. It was designed by I. M. Pei as the new entrance to the Louvre Museum.

The pyramid is made of glass and steel. When it was first built, many people complained. They thought it looked out of place next to the old museum building. Others say it mixes old and new styles in a good way.

Louvre Pyramid
Location: Paris, France
Height: 70 feet (21 meters)
That's Amazing!
This pyramid is made of almost 700 separate pieces of glass.

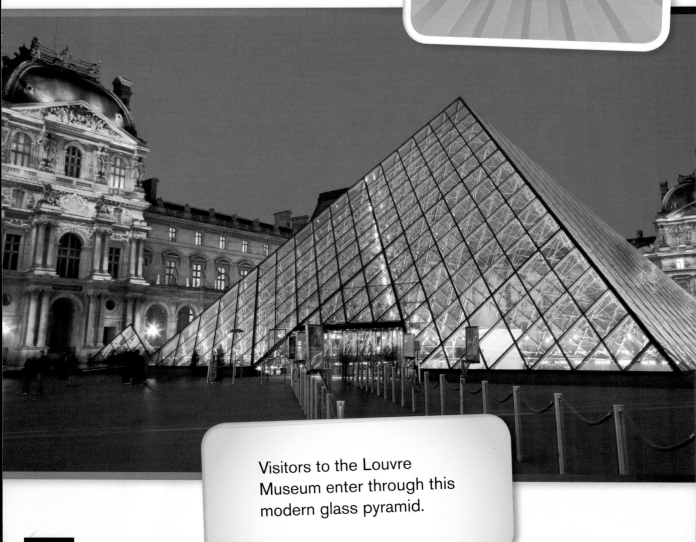

Visitors to the Louvre Museum enter through this modern glass pyramid.

La Pyramide Inversée ("the upside-down pyramid") was also designed by I. M. Pei.

Pyramid structure

There are actually several glass pyramids in and around the Louvre. Three smaller pyramids surround the entrance pyramid. Inside a nearby underground shopping mall, an upside-down glass pyramid serves as a skylight. Underneath stands a small stone pyramid. The tips of each pyramid almost touch.

"Great White Pyramid"

A U.S. pilot was flying over China in 1945. He saw an amazing sight: a huge white pyramid! No one had ever heard of a great pyramid in China. A newspaper article reported the story. But the pilot's description of what he saw did not match the photo included in the article. The pilot said that the pyramid he saw was in the mountains. The photo showed a pyramid in a flat area. The Chinese government said there was no "great white pyramid" anywhere in their country.

"Great White Pyramid"
(Maoling Mausoleum)
Location: Xian, China
Height: 153 feet (46.5 meters)
That's Amazing!
No one expected to find great pyramids in China.

Chinese pyramids are made of mud and earth, with flat tops.

Mystery solved!

The pyramid is now known as the Maoling **Mausoleum**. It is the **tomb** of the Chinese Emperor Wudi, who ruled more than 2,000 years ago. His tomb took 53 years to build.

Other pyramids have now been found in the same region of China—around 38 in total. All are believed to be the burial mounds of early Chinese emperors and their relatives.

The Emperor Wudi is considered to be one of the greatest emperors in Chinese history. Many amazing objects were found inside the pyramid, including this carved stone figure of an ox.

New Pyramid Discoveries

Some of the biggest ancient pyramids are in the jungle of northern Guatemala. This area was home to the ancient Mayan people more than 2,200 years ago. The largest Mayan city was El Mirador and La Danta was its largest pyramid. El Mirador was abandoned around 150 BCE. The jungle grew over this once great city, hiding it from sight. El Mirador was discovered in 1926, but remained unexplored until recently because of its remote location.

La Danta

Location: Mirador Basin, Guatemala

Height: Approximately 230 feet (70 meters) from the forest floor

That's Amazing!

It could be the biggest pyramid in the world (in terms of volume, not height).

Bosnian Pyramids: Fact or Fiction?

In 2005 an **archaeologist** saw a pyramid-shaped hill in Bosnia. He noticed another one nearby. He is now hoping to prove that these are ancient human-made pyramids. If he is correct, these would be the first pyramids discovered in Europe. Most scientists, however, do not believe the Bosnian pyramids are real.

Some people believe Visocica Hill (right) in Bosnia is a 12,000-year-old step pyramid.

Pyramids in Danger

In ancient Egypt, **looters** destroyed pyramids as they looked for treasures buried with the **pharaohs**. Modern looters are still a threat to pyramids, especially those that are still being **excavated**.

Huaca Larga

Huaca Larga, or "long pyramid," is one of 26 major pyramids at Tucume in Peru. The Tucume pyramids were made from sun-baked mud bricks called adobe. Now, most are so worn away that it is hard to tell they were once pyramids.

Huaca Larga is 65 feet (20 meters) high. Experts think it may have been three times as high when it was first built in around 1100.

A ziggurat is a multi-storied pyramid that has a temple on top.

The Great Ziggurat at Ur

The Great Ziggurat in Ur, southern Iraq, is a massive step pyramid that was produced by the ancient Sumerian culture of Mesopotamia. It was completed around 2100 BCE. Modern wars threaten to destroy this amazing **relic**. Rocket and shellfire have damaged the brickwork. Soldiers are suspected of looting at the site, too.

Pyramids Facts and Figures

Pyramids have a flat base with triangle-shaped sides that meet at the top. Some pyramids were built as enormous **tombs** for powerful Egyptian kings. Others had temples on top where people were **sacrificed** to Aztec and Mayan gods. Which pyramid do you think is the most amazing?

Khufu's Pyramid (The Great Pyramid of Giza)

Location: Giza, Egypt

Height: 481 feet (147 meters)

That's Amazing!

The Great Pyramid of Giza is the only one of the **Seven Wonders of the Ancient World** still standing today.

Djoser's (Zoser's) Pyramid

Location: Saqqara, Egypt

Size: Originally 203 feet (62 meters) tall

That's Amazing!

This pyramid is the oldest stone building in Egypt.

Pyramid of the Sun

Location: Near Mexico City, Mexico

Height: 216 feet (66 meters)

That's Amazing!

It's the second-largest pyramid in Central America, the third-largest in the world, and the largest pyramid to be restored in the **Western Hemisphere**.

Pyramid of Kukulcán

Location: Chitchen Itza, Mexico

Height: Approximately 79 feet (24 meters)

That's Amazing!

This pyramid is also a huge stone calendar!

Pyramid of Inscriptions

Location: Palenque, Chiapas, Mexico

Size: 197 feet (60 meters) wide and 89 feet (27 meters) tall

That's Amazing!

Experts studied this pyramid for 200 years before discovering the hidden tomb of a Mayan king.

El Templo Mayor

Location: Mexico City, Mexico

Size: Approximately 330 x 260 feet (100 x 80 meters) at its base

That's Amazing!

The Spanish destroyed this pyramid in 1521 and built a new city on top of the site.

Los Guachimontones

Location: Jalisco, Mexico

Height: 60 feet (18 meters)

That's Amazing!

This is the largest round pyramid in Mexico.

Louvre Pyramid

Location: Paris, France

Height: 70 feet (21 meters)

That's Amazing!

This pyramid is made of almost 700 separate pieces of glass.

"Great White Pyramid" (Maoling Mausoleum)

Location: Xian, China

Height: 153 feet (46.5 meters)

That's Amazing!

No one expected to find great pyramids in China.

La Danta

Location: Mirador Basin, Guatemala

Height: Approximately 230 feet (70 meters) from the forest floor

That's Amazing!

It could be the biggest pyramid in the world (in terms of volume, not height).

Glossary

archaeologist someone who studies ancient remains

equinox two days of the year (on or about March 20 and September 22) when most of the world has the same amount of daylight

excavation action of digging up ancient remains; to excavate means to dig up

inscription words carved into stone or some other surface

looter someone who steals valuable items from somewhere, often during times of war

mausoleum building that contains one or more tombs

mummification process of creating a mummy from the dead body of a person or animal

pharaoh Egyptian king

relic something from long ago that survived when the rest is gone

ritual traditional way of doing something special, usually to do with a religion

sacred connected with religion

sacrifice give up something valuable, such as one's own life

sarcophagus ancient stone coffin, usually decorated with carvings

Seven Wonders of the Ancient World list of seven ancient structures originally recorded by a Greek traveler more than 2,000 years ago

solstice two days each year (on or about June 21 and December 21) when the Sun is closest to the north or south poles

tomb grave, cave, or other place where a dead body is buried

Western Hemisphere half of planet Earth that includes the Americas and parts of western Europe and Africa

World Heritage Site place of outstanding historical value

Books

Chambers, Catherine. *Egyptian Treasures*. New York, NY: Crabtree, 2011.

Down, David. *The Archaeology Book*. Green Forest, AR: Master Books, 2010.

Harris, Nicholas. *Pyramids Through Time*. New York, NY: PowerKids, 2009.

MacDonald, Fiona. *Solving the Mysteries of the Pyramids*. New York, NY: Marshall Cavendish Benchmark, 2009.

Maloy, Jackie. *The Ancient Maya*. New York, NY: Children's Press, 2010.

Websites

http://www.history.com/topics/the-egyptian-pyramids
This History Channel website has videos and photo galleries.

http://www.historyforkids.org/learn/southamerica/before 1500/history/maya.htm
Visit this website to learn more about the temples and pyramids of South America.

http://kids.nationalgeographic.com/kids/stories/history/ ancient-wonders
This website is about the ancient wonders of the world, including the Great Pyramid of Giza—the only one of the ancient wonders still standing.

Index